FOR US

For Us

30-Day Easter Devotional

Erwin W. Lutzer

Moody Church Media
Chicago

Cover by Bryan Butler

FOR US
Copyright © 2025 by Erwin W. Lutzer
Published by Moody Church Media
Chicago, Illinois 60614
www.moodymedia.org

ISBN: 9798306592039

Access Pastor Erwin Lutzer's
six-part series, For Us,
originally preached in 2009.

moodymedia.org/for-us
Listen to Pastor Lutzer's entire series.

INTRODUCTION

For Us—Meditations at the Foot of the Cross

"And if Christ has not been raised, your faith is futile and you are still in your sins....If in Christ we have hope in this life only, we are of all people most to be pitied." —1 Corinthians 15:17, 19

That's right, he said *pitied*. If Christ did not die on the cross and rise again, Christians are in the sad position of being aware of the severity of our sin—and having no remedy for it. Pitiful!

But the miracle of all miracles did happen. He did die for us and He did rise again on the third day!

I wrote this series of 30 devotional meditations to help you approach God in awe, humility, and gratitude. Let's take the lessons we learn from Christ's last earthly hours and His resurrection into our daily lives.

Come with me to the foot of the cross and beyond!

Erwin W. Lutzer

DAY 1

Read

Mark 14:32–34

Here in Gethsemane, we have the gift of seeing Jesus' humanity most clearly. He was "greatly distressed and troubled," going through emotional turbulence so painful He couldn't even stand up under it. He knew He was about to have the full wrath of God unleashed upon Him because of your sin and mine. Completely sinless Himself, He dreaded that onslaught of sin laid on Him.

Do we understand this? When we suffer, Jesus is never far off. He knows. Whatever tragedy has happened in your life, He knows. He has "been made like [us] in every respect," so that you and I never have to suffer alone. That was part of God's plan—to give us a Savior unlike anything in any other religion, a Savior who understands everything because He has experienced everything, yet without sinning. Friends and family may desert us in our time of need, but Jesus is always there bearing our sorrow right along with us. What a friend we have in Jesus, indeed!

Reflect

Hebrews 2:17

Therefore he had to be made like his brothers in every respect, so that he might become a merciful and faithful high priest in the service of God, to make propitiation for the sins of the people.

Notes

Pray

Father, thank you for giving me a Savior who always understands. When trials come, help me remember that Jesus has compassion for my sorrow and I don't have to bear it alone.

In Jesus' name, Amen.

DAY 2

Read
Mark 14:35–36

The Jews and Romans crucified Jesus. He laid down His life for our sin. But ultimately, God was responsible for the death of Jesus. God could have sent legions of angels to "remove the cup" and rescue Jesus—but both Father and Son knew this horrible death was the only way to rescue you and me. They were willing to endure it because they both loved us so much.

Do you think your troubles come only from the devil or from the malice of others? That's the path of bitterness and cynicism. We must grasp the fact that some troubles are part of God's plan to purify and change us. You and I can endure whatever comes our way—remembering the Son walks beside us, the Spirit upholds us, and the Father will not let us suffer one bit beyond what we can bear with His help. Don't focus on your pain, focus on God's purpose for you and the joy He has waiting for us on the other side!

Reflect
Hebrews 12:1–2

Let us run with endurance the race that is set before us, looking to Jesus, the founder and perfecter of our faith, who for the joy that was set before him endured the cross, despising the shame, and is seated at the right hand of the throne of God.

Notes

Pray

Father, help me to recognize the suffering that comes my way as part of your plan to perfect me, and endure it with your strength so I can reach the joy that's set before me.

In Jesus' name, Amen.

DAY 3

Read

Mark 14:35–36

Humanly speaking, Jesus didn't want to die on the cross. Despite His fears, He still said to His Father, "Not what I will, but what you will."

Sometimes we have to do the will of God whether we like it or not. We live in a society where "feeling bad" is a sin we must avoid at all costs. But Jesus shows us that's not God's way. Being filled with the Spirit doesn't mean we'll be happy all the time. We can be anxious or troubled. Like Jesus in Gethsemane, we can be so filled with dread we fall on our faces in fear. But we must trust God and do the right thing. "Your will, not mine," can still be our battle cry.

If Jesus had taken the easy way out, you and I would be trapped in our sins forever. There are times you have to say "no" to your emotions, submit to God's plan, and simply trust Him for the glad day to come.

Reflect

1 Peter 4:13

But rejoice insofar as you share Christ's sufferings, that you may also rejoice and be glad when his glory is revealed.

Notes

Pray

Father, thank you for the example of Jesus' submission to you. Help me to distinguish between my feelings and your will, and give me the strength to choose your will even when it's hard.

In Jesus' name, Amen.

DAY 4

Read
Matthew 26:6–16

Why did Judas betray Jesus? For three years he was a full-fledged disciple, doing miracles, preaching to the people. He appeared to love Jesus. He probably even thought he loved Jesus. But he loved money more, so when "crunch time" came, he chose his greater love: thirty pieces of silver. What a worthless exchange for any life, still less the Son of God!

We can't be too scornful of Judas. We all have the potential for great evil in our hearts, and we all have a tendency to put lesser things, particularly money, before God. Some of the things we choose may even be good, like helping the poor or being active in the church. But if we put them before Jesus, if we let them have our heart, we've fallen into the Judas trap.

Examine your heart. Have you placed anything above Jesus Christ? Have you, in your own way, kissed Him and sent Him away to be crucified?

Reflect
Luke 16:13

No servant can serve two masters, for either he will hate the one and love the other, or he will be devoted to the one and despise the other. You cannot serve God and money.

Notes

Pray

Father, I've let other things creep into my heart where Jesus should be. Help me be on the alert to weed out those things and serve only one master, my Lord and my God.

In Jesus' name, Amen.

DAY 5

Read
Matthew 27:3–10

Judas knew he'd done wrong—we always do, don't we? So out of guilt, he took the silver back to the chief priests and elders. Notice that these men, who were so friendly when Judas could be of use to them, now said, "What's that to us?" and sent him away still full of remorse.

Judas responded to his sorrow in the wrong way. If all we do with our sin is grieve about it and try to make amends in our own way, we'll end up in despair just as Judas did. Right now inside you, worldly sorrow may be eating away and keeping you from taking your sin to Christ, where it belongs.

Regret will keep you looking backward forever and cheat you into thinking there's no hope. It may not kill you physically, but it can paralyze and kill you spiritually. Only repentance before Christ can free you from the past and bring you eternal life.

Reflect
2 Corinthians 7:10

For godly grief produces a repentance that leads to salvation without regret, whereas worldly grief produces death.

Notes

Pray

Father, help me to see that Jesus Christ is the cure for all sin, and to give every sin up to Him so that I can be free. And help me never to give up on anyone's salvation, remembering that you can save anyone, no matter what they've done.

In Jesus' name, Amen.

DAY 7

Read
John 18:12–19:16

Jesus had six trials before His crucifixion, and not one of them was fair. Hired witnesses, violence, judges doing double-duty as prosecutors—never has the phrase "travesty of justice" been more true.

How did Jesus respond? He knew He would never have a fair trial; a fair trial would never have condemned Him to death. But He was willing to trust God's justice in God's time, so He said in effect, "All of these injustices are going to be retried in heaven and my faith is so great I don't need to see justice on Earth."

You and I don't always get justice, do we? Not here on Earth, surrounded by fallen man. When human justice fails, let's take our example from Jesus. Remember that injustice on Earth never escapes God's attention. Instead of saying, "God, move over, I'm going to even the score in my own way," let's conquer bitterness and entrust ourselves to Him who always "judges justly."

Reflect
1 Peter 2:23

When he was reviled, he did not revile in return; when he suffered, he did not threaten, but continued entrusting himself to him who judges justly.

THE JUSTICE OF MAN

Notes

Pray

Father, sometimes I really do want revenge on people who've wronged me. Help me turn that desire over to you and wait patiently for the day you will administer your perfect justice, because you will do it so much better than I could!

In Jesus' name, Amen.

DAY 8

Read

Acts 2:22–24

Jesus' trials were unjust, but they weren't about to derail God's plan. In fact, God used injustice to get Jesus crucified. That's not to say injustice is ever a good thing; indeed, if we find it in ourselves, we must repent immediately. Like Judas, woe to those people who were Satan's tools in the death of Christ!

But when evil comes against us, we can take the example of Jesus' trials, along with the story of Joseph and many others in Bible, to remind us that what some people mean for evil, God means for good.

Maybe you're suffering from an injustice right now. Maybe someone has come up against you with evil in their heart. God knows and sees your suffering. Jesus understands how you feel. The Holy Spirit is with you. Persevere, seek God's justice, and look forward to the day He turns this all to your good.

Reflect

Genesis 50:20

As for you, you meant evil against me, but God meant it for good, to bring it about that many people should be kept alive, as they are today.

THOSE WHO MEAN EVIL

Notes

Pray

Father, you know what my enemies have in mind, how they have evil stored up to do me harm. I give the situation to you right now, knowing their plans are only a tiny part of your plan for my good.

In Jesus' name, Amen.

DAY 9

Read

Luke 23:32–38

"Father, forgive them, for they know not what they do."

How could He even say it? With nails piercing His hands and feet, hanging on the cross with His lungs straining for air—how could that be the first thing that came to His mind? The Greek text implies He didn't just say it once, He repeated it over and over. "Father, forgive them, forgive them, forgive them." Right in the midst of His agony, Jesus prayed for the benefit of His tormentors. What unimaginable mercy! But for Jesus, God's plan was more important than His own suffering.

How long does it take you to forgive someone who hurts you? It's not easy to do. Our own pain tends to consume us, and doesn't leave much room for anyone else's feelings—especially not the person who caused the pain in the first place. Have you hardened your heart against someone and refused to forgive them? Let today be the day you follow Christ's example and say, "Yes, I forgive."

Reflect

Luke 17:4

If he sins against you seven times in the day, and turns to you seven times, saying, "I repent," you must forgive him.

Notes

Pray

Father, forgiveness isn't easy for me. When I'm hurt, I want to hurt back. Help me to feel your Son's tenderness towards those who cause me pain, and learn to forgive when I am wronged.

In Jesus' name, Amen.

DAY 10

Read
Matthew 27:39–44

"Father, forgive them, for they know not what they do."

Have you ever justified yourself, "Well, it's just a tiny sin, not a bad one?" When we do that, you and I are one with the mockers who treated Jesus' death with contempt—the people He prayed for on the cross.

Looked at in one way, we are actually worse. Those who crucified Jesus knew they were doing wrong, but they didn't know the full extent of their sin. They didn't know He really was the Son of God. You and I do, and we have less excuse when we don't take sin seriously—sin that nailed Christ up there on the cross. And with our greater knowledge comes greater judgment, unless of course, we throw ourselves on His mercy and receive His forgiveness.

So read the words of Jesus again. Thank Him that, even as your every sin kept Him nailed to the cross, He cared enough for you to pray that "just retribution" would not come to you.

Reflect
Hebrews 2:2–3

For since the message declared by angels proved to be reliable, and every transgression or disobedience received a just retribution, how shall we escape if we neglect such a great salvation?

WHO MOCKS JESUS?

Notes

Pray

Father, I can't begin to understand the mercy that cried out to save me even while my sin caused Jesus so much pain. Forgive me for every time I've treated sin lightly, and help me remember what it cost Him.

In Jesus' name, Amen.

DAY 11

Read

Acts 3:11—26

"Father, forgive them, for they know not what they do."

Was this prayer answered? We must realize this was not a blanket prayer for everyone involved in Christ's crucifixion; not everyone who participated in this crime was forgiven. But Jesus foreknew that many of those who put Him to death would, indeed, later repent, and He prayed God would let His blood cover their sin. God forgives those who ask. Yes, the prayer was answered for those for whom it was intended.

You and I don't know which of our enemies will repent. But we're called to pray for all who hurt us, even those who don't ask for our forgiveness. Maybe our prayers will be part of their salvation story. In the meantime, we free ourselves from the pain of their attacks by surrendering the matter to God. Remember, forgiveness doesn't have to mean reconciliation. Sometimes it just means letting go.

What old emotional injury are you carrying today from someone who hurt you and never asked forgiveness? Will you give that pain to God and let Him heal the wound? Jesus did not die bitter, and neither should we.

Reflect

Matthew 5:44

But I say to you, Love your enemies and pray for those who persecute you.

FREEDOM IN FORGIVENESS

Notes

Pray

Father, I've been carrying this pain around so long and I don't want it any more. Help me forgive the person who hurt me. Cleanse my heart from angry, bitter thoughts, so that I can better focus on you.

In Jesus' name, Amen.

DAY 12

Read

Luke 23:39–43

"Truly, I say to you, today you will be with me in paradise."

The Bible doesn't elaborate on his crimes. He's just a common thief who, at first, joined in the mockery against Jesus. Observing Jesus' behavior as the crowd taunted "The King of the Jews" planted a seed. With a few of his precious last breaths, he humbly begged Christ to think of him.

The thief admitted he was being punished justly. If we'd known him, we might have said, "Serves him right." Let us remember that we are also thieves. God gives us life and everything we possess, and yet we go off and serve our own interests. This small, tender story reminds us we are just as guilty and helpless. But helplessness isn't a curse if it draws us to the only One who can help us.

Are we robbing God by using His gifts selfishly? Take your example from the repentant thief, and have your sin forgiven by Jesus. Though guilty of the same sin, we can be in paradise!

Reflect

1 Chronicles 29:14, 16

For all things come from you, and of your own have we given you…O LORD our God, all this abundance that we have provided for building you a house for your holy name comes from your hand and is all your own.

Notes

Pray

Father, too often I forget you've given me everything I have, and I rob you of your due glory and honor. Forgive me. Help me recognize and overcome my selfishness.

In Jesus' name, Amen.

DAY 13

Read

Isaiah 53

"Truly, I say to you, today you will be with me in paradise."

When He said those words, Jesus didn't look much like He could fulfill them. Isaiah 53 paints a graphic picture: crushed, stricken, with no beauty or majesty in His physical form. We can only imagine the blood matted into His hair, the raw flesh, the struggles for breath. He was "numbered with the transgressors," and the crowd thought He deserved it.

No wonder the cross is "a stumbling block to Jews and folly to Gentiles." Who would expect—or respect—a Messiah like that? But the repentant thief cried out to Him right in front of that mocking crowd.

Our world would like us to believe the story of Christ's death and resurrection is silly, only for the ignorant. They'd like us to be ashamed of Him. And it would be a strange story, if we had only the wisdom of man. Thank God we have His wisdom through the Holy Spirit, to see how far His grace outstrips all understanding!

Reflect

1 Corinthians 1:23, 25

But we preach Christ crucified, a stumbling block to Jews and folly to Gentiles...For the foolishness of God is wiser than men, and the weakness of God is stronger than men.

Notes

Pray

Father, I never want to be ashamed of Jesus' name. Help me to be bold in claiming Him as my Savior, no matter what the doubting world may say.

In Jesus' precious name, Amen.

DAY 14

Read

Luke 23:39–43

"Truly, I say to you, today you will be with me in paradise."

Do you realize that both thieves offer up a prayer? The unrepentant thief said, "If you are the Christ, save yourself and us." That's a prayer. He wasn't so concerned about eternity. He said, "Just get me off this cross." He prayed and yet was lost forever, because he cared only for physical deliverance in the here and now.

One thief hung on Jesus' right, the other on His left. Both thieves were guilty of their crimes, sentenced to the same death. The only difference between them is how they responded to Jesus.

And just as the cross of Christ stood between them on Skull Hill, it continues to divide all mankind today into the saved and unsaved. By telling this story during the most important moments in the Bible, God shows us that our relationship with Jesus determines our eternal destiny. Everything depends on how you answer the question: "What will I do about Jesus?"

Reflect

Matthew 12:30

Whoever is not with me is against me, and whoever does not gather with me scatters.

Notes

Pray

Father, help me overcome my love for the things of this world, and concentrate on Christ and my eternal future. Help me say with the repentant thief, "Jesus, remember me."

In Jesus' name, Amen.

DAY 15

Read
John 19:23–27

"Woman, behold, your son!"

I wonder if Mary thought of Simeon's words as she stood at the foot of the cross. If she hadn't understood them before, she did now, all too painfully. And when she heard Jesus tell John to assume His duties as eldest son, the last shred of hope disappeared. He was, really and truly, going to die before her eyes.

If you've ever had to stand by and see your own child go through suffering you can't relieve, you know Mary's pain. She would have given anything to stop the crucifixion or trade places with Him, but she knew only His death would purchase her salvation and ours.

Mary couldn't help her Son, but she could be there in patient love. All too often, we choose to avoid the pain of others, especially when it appears that we can do nothing for them. Who do you know today who needs your patient love far more than your advice?

Reflect
Luke 2:34–35

And Simeon blessed them and said to Mary his mother, "Behold, this child is appointed for the fall and rising of many in Israel, and for a sign that is opposed (and a sword will pierce through your own soul also)."

Notes

Pray

Father, thank you for a Savior so tender He thought of His mother even in His agony. Help me to be like Mary, standing at the foot of the cross in patient love for the suffering people in my own life.

In Jesus' name, Amen.

DAY 16

Read
Mark 10:35–45

"Behold, your mother!"

When Jesus was arrested, the disciples all fled in terror and shame. The only one at the foot of the cross that day was John. Apparently, he also had fled. Imagine his guilt as he slunk back to the One he'd promised to serve—the One in whose kingdom he'd hoped to be exalted!

Now, imagine his incredulous joy, even at such a painful time, when Jesus entrusted Mary to him. Those few words told him everything. He was forgiven. He was still loved. And he was to care for someone precious to Jesus. His immediate response made it clear he'd given up all thoughts of being exalted and was glad to serve any way he was asked.

Who has your Savior entrusted to you beyond your immediate family? A young man or woman from a non-believing home to mentor, a bedridden saint to visit, a single parent to comfort and help? Look around with John's eyes today and behold your new family members!

Reflect
Mark 3:34–35

Here are my mother and my brothers! For whoever does the will of God, he is my brother and sister and mother.

A DISCIPLE'S DUTY

Notes

Pray

Father, I want to serve you. Show me those brothers and sisters, fathers and mothers I didn't know I had, and help me find ways to minister your love to them.

In Jesus' name, Amen.

DAY 17

Read
Matthew 27:45-46

"My God, my God, why have you forsaken me?"

No longer does Jesus say, "Father." Into the thick, unnatural darkness that covered the land during the last three hours of His dying, He cries out to express His pain at separation from God. But still He says, "My God," trusting even through despair.

This was the moment when the full weight of our sin dropped squarely on His shoulders. Imagine the punishment for the sins of even one life. Now try to imagine the punishment for millions of lives, for crimes too disgusting even to name. Jesus lived through an eternity of hell compressed into three short hours. But the worst part was the separation from His Father's love and company, which was eternally His greatest delight. The physical darkness mirrored the darkness of His soul cut off from the Light.

This is what Christ willingly suffered so you and I would be spared. What else can we do but stand amazed at such mingled horror and grace?

Reflect
Nahum 1:6

Who can stand before his indignation? Who can endure the heat of his anger? His wrath is poured out like fire, and the rocks are broken into pieces by him.

A FORSAKEN SON

Notes

Pray

Father, I can't even comprehend the intense pain Christ suffered because He loves me. All I can do is offer my heart and my life in gratitude. There is nothing to do but praise you.

In Jesus' name, Amen.

DAY 18

Read

Mark 15:33–34

"My God, my God, why have you forsaken me?"

If Mary's heart was wrung at the foot of the cross, how much more anguish was in the heart of the Father! This was the Son in whom He was "well pleased," the Son with whom He had communed from before the beginning of time. Now the Father had to watch that Son die in agony.

But that was His choice. God chose to suffer. He chose to redeem humanity through the suffering of His Son. Because He loves us.

God didn't suddenly start loving us after the crucifixion. He didn't suddenly go from being a wrathful Old Testament God to a merciful New Testament God. Jesus didn't think up the plan of salvation and "go it alone." Salvation came because our Father is a redeeming God who loves us. The Father and Son took the initiative of redemption together from all eternity. What wondrous love!

Reflect

John 3:16

For God so loved the world, that he gave his only Son, that whoever believes in him should not perish but have eternal life.

Notes

Pray

Father, I admit sometimes I think of you as only a Judge, waiting to punish me for my sins. Help me to remember that you gave your Son willingly out of love for me so that I could truly call you "Father."

In Jesus' name, Amen.

DAY 19

Read
Psalm 22:1–11

"My God, my God, why have you forsaken me?"

Did the Father really forsake the Son on the cross, or did Jesus only feel forsaken? Did He suffer only as a man, as some people suggest, or did He suffer as God?

It is necessary for a holy God to turn His face away from sin. He turned His face away from Jesus, His Son, while He bore our sin. And He will turn His face away from every sinner who comes to the Judgment Seat on their own merits. Jesus chose to be truly forsaken so that we might become acceptable to God, unholy as we are.

If Christ suffered and died only as a man, the Incarnation is a sham and so is our salvation. We must try to grasp the fact that Jesus suffered and died as the God-Man; yes, God suffered too. Obviously God did not and cannot die, but the break in fellowship between the Father and the Son proved that the Godhead was involved in securing our redemption. Salvation is of the Lord!

Reflect
2 Corinthians 5:18–19

All this is from God, who through Christ reconciled us to himself and gave us the ministry of reconciliation; that is, in Christ God was reconciling the world to himself.

WHO DIED ON THE CROSS?

Notes

Pray

Father, I don't fully understand how Jesus could die for me, but I stand firm on this mystery knowing your wisdom is greater than mine. Thank you for loving me so much.

In Jesus' name, Amen.

DAY 20

Read
John 19:28–29

"I thirst."

After all His suffering, of course He was thirsty! A part of the anguish of crucifixion is the dehydration of the body. But why force His tortured body to say the words aloud? John makes it clear His primary purpose was to fulfill the prophecy of Psalm 69:21, "and for my thirst they gave me sour wine to drink."

These two little words, "I thirst" show us that Jesus was fully human on the cross and they challenge us. Would we have run to quench His thirst if we had been at the foot of the cross? We'd like to think so. But how often have we failed to ease the suffering of the "least of these?"

Jesus tells us that to care for our brother or sister in Christ is the same as caring for Him. Isn't that worth whatever it costs us in time, energy, and resources? We shouldn't drag our feet when we see someone in need—we should run to help!

Reflect
Matthew 25:35, 40

For I was hungry and you gave me food, I was thirsty and you gave me drink, I was a stranger and you welcomed me…Truly, I say to you, as you did it to one of the least of these my brothers, you did it to me.

Notes

Pray

Father, sometimes I get wrapped up in my own needs and don't see my brothers and sisters suffering. Help me be more sensitive, and to view everything I do for them as a gift I gladly give to you.

In Jesus' name, Amen.

DAY 21

Read
John 4:4–26

"I thirst."

The One who called Himself the Living Water is thirsty—what irony! Jesus has given up the privileges of deity to drink the "cup of wrath" prepared for Him at full strength. He would do no miracle here to spare Himself one tiny bit of punishment for our sins.

But I think this was more than physical thirst. We're all born with an emptiness inside that can only be filled by God. The Bible often compares it to thirst. For the first time in His life—the first and only time in eternity—Jesus is separated from God and feels that longing. He thirsts.

Our world offers us so many vain ways to satisfy that emptiness we've all felt. Take a good, hard look at your life today. Have you tried to fill your longing with security, money, human love, or anything other than God? What has it cost you in pain and disappointment? Turn back and drink freely from the well of Living Water!

Reflect
Revelation 22:17

The Spirit and the Bride say, "Come." And let the one who hears say, "Come." And let the one who is thirsty come; let the one who desires take the water of life without price.

Notes

Pray

Father, I know only you can truly quench my soul's thirst. Help me put aside the other things I once thought would fill me up and concentrate on being filled by you.

In Jesus' name, Amen.

DAY 22

Read
Mark 15:37–38; John 19:30

"It is finished."

In Greek, this cry of Jesus is one word, *tetelestai,* and in legal terms it could also mean "paid in full." Jesus wants us to know that our sins are paid in full. There is not one little bit left to "make up."

That's good, because you or I can, at best, manage our sin; we cannot pay for it. With one word, Jesus destroys "works righteousness"—the idea that we can help save ourselves through our own good works. The gulf between our impurity and God's holiness is too vast. As commendable as good works are, they mean nothing when it comes to receiving the gift of our salvation.

If you have received Christ, your sins are paid in full. Yes, our sins are paid for, both past and future. Yes, we still must confess those sins God brings to our attention to stay in fellowship with Him, but the record of our sins is a blank page in heaven! Wonderful thought!

Reflect
Colossians 2:13–14

And you, who were dead in your trespasses and the uncircumcision of your flesh, God made alive together with him, having forgiven us all our trespasses, by canceling the record of debt that stood against us with its legal demands. This he set aside, nailing it to the cross.

Notes

Pray

Father, forgive me for sometimes thinking that I just need to "be a good person" to earn your favor. Help me remember that I am acceptable to you only when I'm clothed in Christ's righteousness.

In Jesus' name, Amen.

DAY 23

Read
Hebrews 9

"It is finished."

Jesus came to Earth with a task: to suffer, preach, heal, and die. In the midst of the crucifixion ordeal, He cried out in triumph that He had fulfilled His mission to the last detail. There was nothing He left undone, nothing to regret.

The heavy curtain separating the Most Holy Place from the rest of the temple was torn in two. No longer would a high priest need to go in with the blood of animals. That covenant was over forever. The doorway to the Most Holy Place stood open to all.

Unlike Jesus, we don't always clearly see the task God has for us, and we don't know when we will die. All the more reason to keep our eyes wide open, looking for opportunities to do God's will. Live today so that you, too, can say, "it is finished" in your final hour—and look forward to hearing, "Well done, good and faithful servant."

Reflect
Hebrews 10:12, 14

But when Christ had offered for all time a single sacrifice for sins, he sat down at the right hand of God…For by a single offering he has perfected for all time those who are being sanctified.

THE TORN CURTAIN

Notes

Pray

Father, there are times I don't see the task you have for me. There are times I willfully choose not to do the tasks I see. Help me to delight in your will and work for a life that will finish with nothing left undone!

In Jesus' name, Amen.

DAY 24

Read
Luke 23:46

"Father, into your hands I commit my spirit!"

Jesus' life wasn't taken from Him. He delivered it up at precisely the moment He chose; it was the moment He had suffered the full measure of wrath for our sins. His work was done and now He says "Father" once again, as His Spirit wings its way home.

Hanging on a cross, in unimaginable suffering, beaten and bruised, Jesus was still in control. If He was in control then, how can we imagine He's not in control now, seated with the Father in the fullness of His power?

Jesus knows when your last day will be. God has decided how your end will come. You may have time to gather your friends and family to say farewell. Or, you may be gone in an instant. But if you are in Christ, you do not have to worry about that day. It's in the hands of the One who loves you best. All you have to do is be ready to say, "Here I come, Lord!"

Reflect
John 10:28–29

I give them eternal life, and they will never perish, and no one will snatch them out of my had. My Father, who has given them to me, is greater than all, and no one is able to snatch them out of the Father's hand.

IN THE FATHER'S HANDS

Notes

Pray

Father, I worry about how and when I'm going to die. I fear accidents and illness. I release that fear to you today, acknowledging that every detail of my death is in your loving hands.

In Jesus' name, Amen.

DAY 25 – THE WAY PREPARED

Read

John 14:1–7

"Father, into your hands I commit my spirit!"

Those who haven't accepted Christ's redeeming work have every reason to fear death. Every last affront to God's holiness will be paid for with their personal suffering—for eternity.

But if we have accepted Christ, we have nothing to fear. Jesus has gone ahead of us to prepare the way; and when we die, we'll find Him waiting for us. What could be better? We'll be in heaven, with our own personalities and memories intact, surrounded by those friends who have also accepted Christ—and we'll be sinless, in a place with no tears or sorrow.

This isn't our "eternal reward" for something we've done right. It's Christ's victory over sin and death—His free gift to us. Paul wrote, "When the perishable puts on the imperishable, and the mortal puts on immortality, then shall come to pass the saying that is written: 'Death is swallowed up in victory'" (1 Corinthians 15:54).

Reflect

Revelation 1:17–18

Fear not, I am the first and the last, and the living one. I died, and behold I am alive forevermore, and I have the keys of Death and Hades.

THE WAY PREPARED

Notes

Pray

Father, help me remember that death isn't the end of the road, it's the turning that brings me fully into your presence. Strengthen me to do your work while I live, and grant me joy as I anticipate coming home.

In Jesus' name, Amen.

DAY 26

Read
John 20:1–16

Mary Magdalene stayed at the foot of the cross until the bitter end. She saw where Jesus was laid. After the Sabbath, she was the first one to the tomb, and when she saw it empty, she was so grief-stricken even angels couldn't rouse her hope in the resurrection.

Nor did she recognize Jesus when she saw Him. Looking for a dead body, she couldn't comprehend a live one. Until God opened her eyes.

To see Mary outside the empty tomb is like seeing ourselves. We can stand our whole lives looking at Jesus and never see Him unless God opens our eyes and hearts to the truth about Him. And then we can choose—will we accept Him or not?

When she recognized Him in the garden, Mary fell to her knees and called Him "Master." Her life is a picture of how anyone with a personal and honest relationship with God can go from the depths of sin to being a useful member of God's family.

Reflect
John 1:9–10

The true light, which gives light to everyone, was coming into the world. He was in the world, and the world was made through him, yet the world did not know him.

Notes

Pray

Father, I admit sometimes I don't recognize Jesus in my daily life when He gives me opportunities to encounter Him. Open my eyes so I can see Him clearly and call Him "Master."

In Jesus' name, Amen.

DAY 27

Read
John 20:17–18

What would it be like to be possessed by seven devils? You might recall that when Jesus first met Mary Magdalene, He delivered her from the demons that haunted her body. We don't know how long she lived with these horrid alien beings, but she must have tried everything to escape. Mary knew she couldn't manage her sin or its consequences, on her own. She was ready for her Savior! Salvation comes most easily to the broken. Jesus only has value to us when we're prepared to admit we can't "go it alone."

Jesus lets Mary see Him first after His resurrection, and she tell the disciples about it. He tells her He is going to "my Father and your Father." What better proof that her sins were washed away and she was a beloved daughter of the King!

Have you ever thought, "God can't use me because of my sins?" Or looked down on a brother or sister in Christ because of their past? Mary shows us that once our sins are forgiven, we are equal in God's eyes and able to serve Him equally.

Reflect
Galatians 3:28–29

There is neither Jew nor Greek, there is neither slave nor free, there is no male and female, for you are all one in Christ Jesus. And if you are Christ's, then you are Abraham's offspring, heirs according to promise.

Notes

Pray

Father, cleanse me from regrets and memories of sin that stop me from doing everything you have planned for me, and help me see my brothers and sisters in Christ through your eyes.

In Jesus' name, Amen.

DAY 28

Read
John 14:16–17

"Mary," He said, and she knew from the tender sound of her name that it was Jesus speaking to her. Of course, Mary Magdalene was not married to Jesus, but she had traveled with Him and joined with other women who had a close relationship with Him. When she called Him "Lord" or "Master," she knew who she was talking to.

You and I don't have Jesus here on Earth to walk and talk with. But through the gift of the Holy Spirit and God's Word, we can still have a relationship with Christ as close and personal as Mary did—in fact, if we don't, we will not be saved.

You're not saved because your family is, because you're baptized, or even because you acknowledge Jesus as the Savior. Salvation comes when you accept Him as your Savior, knowing who He is and what He has done *for you*.

You may never hear Him speak your name in this life, but I assure you, if you accept Him as your Savior, you will hear your name in heaven in a voice so tender.

Reflect
John 20:29

Jesus said to him, "Have you believed because you have seen me? Blessed are those who have not seen and yet have believed."

A PERSONAL LOVE

Notes

Pray

Father, thank you for the gift of the Holy Spirit so I can draw close to you. Thank you that, although you created and maintain the whole universe, you also know my name.

In Jesus' name, Amen.

DAY 29

Read
Acts 3:11–4:4

The story of the crucifixion really only affects people in one of two ways.

For some, and I pray you're one of them, the story softens the heart. It makes us aware of the severity of our sin and the boundless love of God. It draws us to salvation for the first time, or makes us reaffirm our commitment to Christ in fear and trembling.

But for others—far too many others—the story hardens the heart. Every time they hear it, some people are more determined than ever not to believe. And each time they turn away, their heart becomes a little more calloused. The path back to God becomes a little more steep. The time may soon come when they have so hardened their hearts and chosen so willfully not to listen, that they simply can't accept Christ. There is nothing sadder.

Every choice you make either brings you closer to God or takes you further away. Which path have you chosen today?

Reflect
Hebrews 4:7

Today, if you hear his voice, do not harden your hearts.

Notes

Pray

Father, I want to draw closer to you. Help me make wise choices and take the steps that will keep my feet on the path of righteousness.

In Jesus' name, Amen.

DAY 30

Read
John 17

Jesus longs to have a personal relationship with you. That's the whole point of His life on Earth and His sacrificial death. God could have accomplished His purposes in some other way, but this was the only way He could be "God with you," adopt you into His family, and show you how much He wants your fellowship.

If you already have a personal relationship with Christ, will you pray this prayer with me today?

"Father, I am amazed at the mystery of salvation. I am amazed at the love you have shown me. Thank you that you tenderly drew me to yourself, showed me my sins, then washed them away. Help me to stand at the foot of the cross in awe every day, offering you my whole life in gratitude for your incomparable gift. In Jesus' name, Amen."

If you haven't yet accepted Christ as your personal sin-bearer, why don't you right here say, "Jesus, I see the gulf between God's holiness and my sinfulness. I see that I can never cross it on my own. Forgive me. Cleanse me. I receive what you did for me as my own. Jesus, remember me when you come into your kingdom."

Reflect
1 John 3:1

See what kind of love the Father has given to us, that we should be called children of God; and so we are.

FROM MY HEART TO YOURS

Notes

DAY	READ	REFLECT
1	Mark 14:32-34	Hebrews 2:17
2	Mark 14:35-36	Hebrews 12:1-2
3	Mark 14:35-36	1 Peter 4:13
4	Matthew 26:6-16	Luke 16:13
5	Matthew 27:3-10	2 Corinthians 7:10
6	Mark 14:41-46	Romans 8:1-2
7	John 18:12-19:16	1 Peter 2:23
8	Acts 2:22-24	Genesis 50:20
9	Luke 23:32-38	Luke 17:4
10	Matthew 27:39-44	Hebrews 2:2-3
11	Acts 3:11-26	Matthew 5:44
12	Luke 23:39-43	1 Chronicles 29:14, 16
13	Isaiah 53	1 Corinthians 1:23, 25
14	Luke 23:39-43	Matthew 12:30
15	John 19:23-27	Luke 2:34-35
16	Mark 10:35-45	Mark 3:34-35
17	Matthew 27:45-46	Nahum 1:6
18	Mark 15:33-34	John 3:16
19	Psalm 22:1-11	2 Corinthians 5:18-19
20	John 19:28-29	Matthew 25:35, 40
21	John 4:4-26	Revelation 22:17
22	Mark 15:37-38; John 19:30	Colossians 2:13-14
23	Hebrews 9	Hebrews 10:12, 14
24	Luke 23:46	John 10:28-29
25	John 14:1-7	Revelation 1:17-18
26	John 20:1-16	John 1:9-10
27	John 20:17-18	Galatians 3:28-29
28	John 14:16-17	John 20:29
29	Acts 3:11-4:4	Hebrews 4:7
30	John 17	1 John 3:1

moodymedia.org/for-us
Share Pastor Lutzer's series with others.